What People Are Saying Ab

"Positive, enthusiastic, insightful & generous - that's Dom. He is a life-long learner, exploring & discovering new knowledge, while at the same time, generously sharing & learning from the lessons life has taught him along the way. In Dom's new book, he shares his experiences & the actions he's found crucial to creating success & an extraordinary life. Throughout the pages, Dom shares his knowledge, stories, & most importantly his heart, to inspire each of us to keep on going & grow into the life we deserve."

- Wendy Elover, Serial Entrepreneur &
Author of "My Cape is At the Cleaners"

"Dom Brightmon has taken thousands of pages of wisdom covering centuries of humanities greatest achievements and is putting his own interpretation on the work and delivering it to you, in the book you are holding in your hands. Be ready to learn, be ready to grow."

- Mike Shelah, LinkedIn Consultant & Keynote Speaker

"In Stay the Course: The Elite Performers 7 Keys to Sustainable Success, Dominique Brightmon provides next-level insights. This is a practical field guide to get you to greatness. Dominique lives his message and practices what he preaches. These tips and strategies are relevant and immediately applicable. Buy this book today and stay the course to your Mountaintop."

- Jeff Davis, author of "Reach Your Mountaintop" and
authentic leadership expert, jeffdspeaks.com

"I highly encourage all winners or future winners to read this book. Dom lays out the best advice on how to achieve your dreams in the most organized and compete fashion. Highly recommend reading this book, as many will be able to relate and learn from it."

- Christy Callahan-Cromwell,
Personal Trainer, Volleyball Coach &
Author of "Top Keys for Weight Loss"

"Stay the Course is a must-read for everyone looking to get to their next level. It is motivational and inspirational. Dom provides quotes and stories that are encouraging and relatable to readers. If you are looking to achieve and maintain your success then Stay the Course is the book for you."

- Christina Alva, Serial Entrepreneur &
Author of "Beyond the Job Description"

STAY THE COURSE

The Elite Performer's 7 Secret
Keys to Sustainable Success

DOMINIQUE B. BRIGHTMON

CONTENTS

DEDICATION

To my wonderful mom Ella Brightmon
and awesome brother Wayne Brightmon.
You both keep me heading north.

ACKNOWLEDGMENTS

Thanks to all of my family, friends and the members of the Mt. Moriah Baptist Church for supporting my 1st book and more importantly, supporting me during my time of grief.

Most of all, thank **you** for picking up and reading this book. Especially those who kept asking me when this book would finally be published. A published author with no audience is merely a human with a published journal.

INTRODUCTION

What is an elite performer? An elite performer is someone who has the mindset to be resilient against all odds and delivers a level of consistent and excellent satisfaction to whatever company they work for (even if it's their own company). Continuously tithe to your dreams. You must dedicate time and count the cost to continue on the path of embracing victories and creating new ones to stay the course.

After publishing my 1st book *Going North*, it landed me TV, podcast, and radio interviews. While the book was opening doors for me, other doors were closing. I lost my father after his 6-year struggle with Alzheimer's, gained 64 lbs. (29 kgs) of weight and was not the same elite performer on my full-time job. This helped me to realize that self-awareness and self-care are the fuel that keeps progress heading north.

"Self-awareness is probably the most important thing towards being a champion."

- Billie Jean King

The tools you will find ahead are the ones that helped me refocus, lose 20 of the total 64 lbs and launch my top-rated podcast that can be heard all over the world in over 50 countries. This book you are reading is a message to those who need encouragement to keep going despite any difficulty. Some of the things you will read may be new to you and some may not. The first five chapters are dedicated to being self-aware in five different areas of life. The last two chapters are for empowerment, encouragement, and expression. North is the direction, staying the course is the action.

CHAPTER 1

Mental Awareness

"Do not be conformed to this world [any longer with its superficial values and customs], but be transformed *and* progressively changed [as you mature spiritually] by the renewing of your mind [focusing on godly values and ethical attitudes], so that you may prove [for yourselves] what the will of God is, that which is good and acceptable and perfect [in His plan and purpose for you]."

Romans 12:2
(AMP)

To stay the course, a reinvention will have to take place to ensure adaptability and longevity. To reinvent yourself, start with your mindset. What gets you going will not always keep you going. A new mindset comes from being aware of certain principles and being introduced to new ones that can yield growth.

To stay on track to northbound success, adopt new actions that provoke favorable odds. Sometimes, changing your view can point you north into a different and better direction.

In-In

The In-In mindset is where you have the mind of a beginner who is ready to absorb ideas and continually grow from each experience through intentional improvement. This was inspired by two Japanese words, *Shoshin* (beginner's mind) & *Kaizen* (continuous improvement).

Let's start with Shoshin. Shoshin is a Japanese term used heavily with meditation in Buddhism. This beginner's mind can be applied to something less spiritual like attending a personal development conference when you don't usually go to conferences or continually asking questions when you are starting a new job.

In a classic story, a bright young student sought to learn about Zen from a Zen master. When the student arrived at the master's home, he sat down for tea and spouted off everything he knew about Zen. While the student was rambling, the philosopher continually poured tea into the student's cup until it ran over. The student yelled, "stop!

the cup is full and no more tea can go in!" Then the master said, you are like that cup. How can you drink of my tea if you already have a full cup? You must empty your cup to receive new tea of wisdom, knowledge, and enlightenment.

We, like the excited student, must learn not to go into certain situations with a full cup (or head) of information and preconceived notions. *We cannot expect to gain anything if we already know "everything".* Have the beginner's mind to accept new knowledge and opportunities to succeed.

> "If your mind is empty, it is always ready for anything, it is open to everything. In the beginner's mind there are many possibilities, but in the expert's mind, there are few."
>
> – Shunryu Suzuki

With opportunities come possibilities to gain and grow. Kaizen is all about growth. Kaizen is translated as continuous improvement. The Toyota Motor company is a company known for decades of elite performance and Kaizen was made popular by them. As of this writing, Toyota is the 12th best-regarded company and 9th most valuable brand in the world according to Forbes.[1] If you are seeking to get back on your personal growth plan, then choose to have a beginner's mind that seeks to continuously grow from all life experiences with the awareness to adjust when necessary.

> "When the status quo becomes your main weapon, your arsenal is diminished. When you can find no other way forward except for repetition, your mistakes are compounded into defeat."
>
> - Georges St. Pierre

Action Steps

1. Do an inventory of your current daily activities and see what can be improved or done differently.

2. Start developing a new and expanded mindset by doing one new thing a day. It can be taking a different route to work, waking up 5 minutes earlier by going to bed 5 mins earlier or greeting one new person a day.

3. Focus on 1 new positive thought daily. This can be done with an affirmation like, "Something wonderful is going to happen to me today", or "I am blessed in many ways for many days."

4. Ask yourself, "What can I do to remain relevant in my field of expertise?" As professional development legend Brian Tracy says, "You must continually raise the bar on yourself."

CHAPTER 2

Time Awareness

"Don't waste your life. It is too short, valuable and irreplaceable."

- Mike Murdock

Everyone has the same amount of time (1,440 minutes a day) but your daily activities determine your effectiveness. Track your expended time by using a tracker or a calendar that goes into 30-minute blocks. If you want to get more technical, go with 10-15 min blocks. When you block your activities into mini activity bricks, you'll see that you might have more time than you think. You could be fooling yourself into the foggy delusion of having no time when all you need to do is lift the fog up by listing the main activities you must accomplish for the day and placing them in the appropriate brick to be completed.

Track your time for a month and see where you spend the time the most. Find ways to lessen the amount of time expended so your reserves of energy can be used on more high return yielding activities. Time management is life management through monitoring the energy you drop on projects and other activities. Brick by brick, you can shatter projects by setting aside the proper amount of time and unbroken focus.

Having a view of where your time goes gives you more clarity on which time bandits are stealing from you. When you find the life thief, you can trip him up and drop him into a daze that can open you up for more activity. Time management is activity management by expending energy on what generates you more success, income, and room for more activities.

"What is the most valuable use of my time right now?"

- Brian Tracy

10 Thoughts about Time

1. Everyone wants a piece of your time, especially if they are selling something.

2. Time is the universal equalizer. We all have the same amount of 86,400 seconds a day.

3. Planning daily can increase your focus.

4. The greatest time bandits on earth are distractions, impatience, laziness, and procrastination.

5. Everyone has time to do something but that "something" may not be seen as a valuable use of their time compared to something else.

6. Asking the right questions can limit the misuse of your time.

7. Not having a goal wastes your time and life.

8. Some things require more time and energy than others in order to have the best possible outcome.

9. Leaders use their time *wisely* to benefit others.

10. Success involves a series of good decisions. The decision you make today can affect your tomorrow.

Action Steps:

1. Invest in a calendar that has a day divided into 30-minute blocks and track your activities for at least 1-month. If that seems like too much, start with 1-week and work your way up to a month.

2. Find the things that are sucking most of your time away daily and shorten the amount of time required to complete that task or get rid of the activity all together if possible.

CHAPTER 3

Influence Awareness

"If I hadn't had mentors, I wouldn't be here today. I'm a product of great mentoring, great coaching... Coaches or mentors are very important. They could be anyone--your husband, other family members, or your boss."

- Indra Nooyi

It's always a good thing to have someone in your corner, whether it's a coach, mentor or trusted friend. The ones around you the most are the ones who will help you become better or worse. Be aware of the people that create your immediate circle of influence.

Have a Crew of Advancement Angels

Legendary 2-time world champion boxer George Foreman had a core group of corner men that kept his career in mind over their own personal agendas. It's been said that great boxers have 3 core people in their corner, a technician, a cut man, and a trainer. A technician knows what obstacles you may face and can guide you on ways to avoid defeat or a very painful learning lesson. The cut man patches up what may be revealed, read a boxers psychological state, and has tools to help you recover from a small injury. The trainer is the one who is around you the most when you prepare for victory. They usually have a handle on your habits and energy levels. Have someone in your corner that is wise enough to see ahead or has a sense of what you need to do to adjust your tactics for success.

"An elite performer has a team around them that has their best interests in mind and seeks the best for them."

- Dominique Brightmon

On my 1st day of school in 7th grade at a new school, I sat by myself after getting lunch since I wasn't good at making friends back then. Time went on and about 10 minutes were left for the lunch period, a guy named John Foster in the 8ᵗʰ grade asked me if I wanted to sit with him and the rest of his friends at his table. I agreed and followed him to a lunch table where I was introduced to John Haggerty and Jordan Russell. Since being connected with them, I gained some friends for a lifetime. They have helped me with what to expect in the next grade, dispensed wisdom, and became a team of supporters.

Who are you connected with? Is your Wi-Fi signal open for other networks of wonderful people? Are you creating links to leverage in your life? *What can you do today to gain the ultimate advantage tomorrow?* Inspect your connections with others and see if you are adding value to them. Those who add value first are valuable because they advance and propel progress.

Champions Have People around Them That Challenge Them

"A mentor is someone who sees more talent and ability within you, than you see in yourself, and helps bring it out of you."

- Bob Proctor

Legendary Mixed Martial Artist and 4-time world champion, Georges St. Pierre had a mentor by the name of Kristof Midoux that encouraged him to become more confident in his fighting ability. Kristof would have a 17-year old Georges fight seasoned professional mixed martial artists that would enhance his fighting ability. Facing these fighters who were tons more powerful than Georges, skyrocketed his confidence because pummeling an obstacle that looks impossible on paper can propel ones inner strength. Be around those who help you to believe in your own God-given power.

Action Steps:

1. Ask yourself, *"who am I surrounding myself with and what are they speaking into my life?"* If you are around negative people, go to different places where positive people hang out. Get around smart and financially responsible people.

2. Seek to be around those who can see the weaknesses that you can't. You may see yourself as invincible, but people may see 3 different weak points where they can strike.

CHAPTER 4

Connection Awareness

"Leaders are born at conferences."

- Mark Victor Hansen

I n a few self-development books, there is an exercise where you write your own obituary. Shortly after writing my own personal obituary, a key to unlocking the 1st door of fulfillment presented itself. That door of fulfillment was to become a published author. In fall 2015, I was attending a conference and having a conversation with one of the attendees during the networking break. During the conversation, I handed her a reading list known as the *100 Books for Dynamic Living*. She looked up and down the list then asked me where my name and book on this list was. When I told her that I was not an author, she dared me to write a book. After not accepting her dare, she offered to join me in the challenge by agreeing to write her book along with me and to have both of them published in one year. I still said no and ended our chat.

A few days later during a Q&A session at a Toastmasters meeting, I declared that I would write and publish a book in one year after someone at the meeting asked me when I was going to write one. I went home that night and wrote like a man possessed and focused on a mission like a paid mercenary. Months went by, and my 1st entry into the business of immortality called *Going North: Tips & Techniques to Advance Yourself* was published. After the book was published, I did a few book signings and started a podcast to keep the brand alive.

My friends saw my efforts, and they too became inspired to write their books. I'm grateful that five of them are now published authors and are continuing to advance themselves. *Let your action be the inspiration that others need.* When you inspire others to do something in their own lives that will help them create a stronger version of themselves, it's called explosive growth. Your display of personal growth will breathe inspiration into others to do something better with themselves.

"If your actions inspire others to dream more, learn more, do more and become more, you are a leader."

- John Quincy Adams

Networking

"Be a source for people."

- Dr. Sinclair Grey III

Seek to connect, not only with others but also with future opportunities to gain and help others. A friend of mine, Mike Shelah has a speech called *The ABC's of LinkedIn* and I love the premise of his speech, "Always be connecting". When you seek to help others, it can come back to you in one form or another. When I was at a book festival selling my book, I was also doing book swaps with some of the other authors at the event. Little did I know that one of the book swaps led to a speaking engagement four months later. Your book can speak for you when you are not awake and available. Always be connecting.

When I was launching my podcast, I sought out to interview authors. My friend, Mike, introduced me to dozens of wonderful people who later became featured on the Going North podcast. This caused a massive amount of recorded interviews being in a backlog because I connected with others and added value to their lives. *Have a cheerful, helpful spirit that welcomes reciprocity.*

After befriending a leadership coach in Toastmasters International, it opened the door of opportunity to speak at a men's leadership conference. When you think of others and help them, karma finds you and rewards you with a reflective gift.

> "You never know how your life can change
> by just saying 'hi' to somebody."
>
> - Dominique Brightmon

Action Steps:

1. Attend a networking event or a conference and start talking to people. You can head to meetup.com or eventbrite.com to find an event that interests you.

2. Follow-up with everyone you meet at the event via email, phone call and or social media.

3. Assist at least one person in one way or another after connecting with them. You become

successful by helping a lot of other people to become successful.

4.   For more detailed networking tips, check out the list in the back of the book titled **Read & Grow Rich.** Especially titles 10, 18, 24, & 26.

CHAPTER 5

Habit Awareness

"Habits are important. Up to 90 percent of our everyday behavior is based on habit. Nearly all of what we do each day, every day, is simply habit."

- Jack D. Hodge

The greatest thing you can do for yourself is to analyze your habits and take an inventory of what needs to change. A desire for change accompanied with deliberate, intentional action yields results.

One major lesson I learned after increasing my workload and production rate is that you have to adjust accordingly to keep yourself at a high level of production. Neglecting sleep, exercise, and other forms of required self-care will leave you empty.

The 50 Billion Dollar Collective Loss

"Sleep is that golden chain that ties health and our bodies together."

- Thomas Dekker

If you have been on the planet long enough, you will hear some people say that they get little sleep to give them an advantage. However, studies show that to be a problem. In a study done by the National Sleep Foundation in 2008, it showed that not getting enough sleep has led to \$16,000,000,000 in annual health care costs and \$50,000,000,000 worth of lost productivity. [1] When you neglect your own well-being by not getting enough sleep, it can yield a cascade of negative events that will appear into your life. Less sleep means reduced awareness, diminished focus, and weight gain.

Move to Keep Moving

"Take care of your body, and it will take care of you."

- Mike Murdock

Working out regularly will be some of the most difficult works that one does in life (depending on your profession). Legendary hall of fame professional wrestler, Shawn Michaels was known for his 5-star matches that would last 45+ minutes. He was told by a wrestler by the name of Tony Faulk in the '80s that wrestling was going to be a "body business" and that it belonged to those who work out. Everybody is in business. Whether it's in the business of staying employed or having the mindset to stay an entrepreneur. Everyone has a body that's in business, and it must be healthy enough to stay the course.

Tony Faulk did not follow his own advice about working out, but Shawn Michaels did. Shawn took the advice of someone who was not qualified to give it but following it paid huge dividends in his career. Shawn realized that the better shape he was in, the better his matches would be. He worked out for 30-60 minutes a day to maintain his cardio for marathon matches that would go for 60 minutes every night for a week. After retirement, Shawn continues to work out to keep his quality of life at a good level. Go for workouts that will increase your quality of life. The benefit of having a workout regimen is that if you do it long enough, it will become routine.

The Power of Prayer

For years since late 2000, my dad would have choking issues and found it hard to swallow food. This led to him losing tons of weight over the years because some days he would go without food because he would just throw it up. My family prayed for years that he would be healed and on a Saturday afternoon celebrating my 14th birthday, my dad testified to us that he had been healed from his choking problem. While he was sharing his testimony, there was a feeling of warmth throughout the table because even though it took a few years, our prayers were finally answered. Since he testified to us, he had not dealt with that choking problem ever again. Prayer works on the hourglass of God and not man. We want everything now, but God wants things done at the appointed time so he can get the glory and receive the appropriate praise.

> "In my deepest, darkest moments, what really got me through was a prayer. Sometimes my prayer was 'Help me.' Sometimes a prayer was 'Thank you.' What I've discovered is that intimate connection and communication with my creator will always get me through because I know my support, my help, is just a prayer away."
>
> - Iyanla Vanzant

7 Tips to a Terrific Morning

"Every single morning takes root the night before."

- Georges St. Pierre

1. Set your goals for the next day in advance during the night before in the form of a written to do list with no more than 6 items on it. The bigger the list, the less you tend to accomplish. You don't want to eat everything at the All You Can Eat buffet.

2. Have your outfit ready the night before to save those precious morning minutes. Sock searching can slap away seconds of go time.

3. Avoid using social media or watching the news when you first wake up in the morning. Check in with yourself first before checking in on the world. Use your morning to get centered. Shut the world out in the morning and get your mind ready for the day.

4. Give yourself 5 minutes or more of silence. Let the snooze button be your timer for sensational

moments of silence. This silence can be a form of meditation.

5. Speak an additional blessing into your day through a prayer of thanks and or saying an affirmation like, "Something good is going to happen to me today."

6. Read or listen to a quick inspirational message. The Bible (specifically Psalms and Proverbs) is a great place to start, and YouTube is full of content.

7. Do a light workout with stretching. I personally do 3 sets of 10 pushups, 10 sit ups, and 10 squats.

"Exercise, prayer, and meditation are examples of calming rituals. They have been shown to induce a happier mood and provide a positive pathway through life's daily frustrations."

- Chuck Norris

A Light Heart Lifts Heavy Burdens

"In this life of brevity, you need levity."

– Dominique Brightmon

A day is not complete without some laughter. The hardest days can have one soft moment that can help you keep pushing forward. Learn to insert more laughter and fun into your daily life. Here are some benefits of laughter. [2]:

- Enhanced levels of creative thinking.
- Improved breathing
- Improved brain function and cardiac health
- Reduced blood pressure levels
- Reduced stress and anxiety.

> "The stresses and demands of daily life often prevent adults from seeing life's abundant hilarity, which is an important component of happiness."
>
> - Dr. Elizabeth Lombardo

Action Steps:

1. Try to get more sleep if you have poor sleeping habits.

2. Insert more body movement and laughter into your daily routine.

3. Add some time for meditation and or prayer into your daily routine if you don't do one or the other.

4. Implement something new into your daily routine that could increase your quality of life. A question to ponder on is, *what am I doing to ensure that I'm around (in human form) as long as possible?*

CHAPTER 6

Gratitude

"There are miracles happening everyday in people's lives. It's just that they don't recognize them for what they are."

- Antoine Garrett

One of the things you will find about the successful people is that they express and show gratitude. Elite performers are those who are grateful for their given abilities to excel and succeed. Gratitude is one of the biggest gifts you can give yourself because it opens the door to receive more.

$30 is not affordable for everybody

"Don't envy anyone because you don't know
how they acquired what they have."

- Dr. Ava Brown

Successful people are grateful because they know that
what they have could be lost and there are others out in
the world who don't have what they have. In episode 79 of
the Going North Podcast, I interviewed a fellow author,
and multi-award winning international speaker Dr. Ava
Brown from the United Kingdom (UK). During our chat,
she mentioned that she was shocked that no one was reg-
istering for one of her $30 events. A friend of hers called
her out on it and said that not everyone can afford $30.
Ava realized that her friend was right because Ava herself
had a rough beginning in Jamaica and only reached her
high level of abundance a couple of years ago at the time
of this writing. It pays to never forget and neglect humble
beginnings because someone out there is going through
that period right now.

Be Grateful for the Gift of Living Loved Ones

While I was in a Toastmasters meeting, we were in the
portion of the meeting called Table Topics. This is where
you get up and speak for 1–2 minutes on a random subject

that you don't know about until it's your turn to speak. When my turn came around, the question I received was, "What 3 people have influenced you the most in your life?" The 1st two persons were easy. My mother & father.

My mother was a smart southern girl who moved to Maryland when she married my dad. Because of her upbringing, she had a southern accent. All of her life, she dedicated herself to becoming an effective communicator and getting rid of her southern accent to become more accepted by others. When I was born, she made sure to always speak well. Thanks to her example, I have become a professional speaker who seeks to inspire others.

My father was a veteran who served for 12 years in the US Army during World War II as a paratrooper in the 82nd Airborne Division, and in the Korean War. He loved music a lot — especially blues, gospel, jazz and more. His music collection was so extensive that the CD's would look like miniature skyscrapers. Within those tune towers, I learned to love music and listen to it daily.

After my time was up, the Topics Master gave me an action step since we were good friends. The action step was to thank those I named. I went to visit my father the next day and thanked him for helping me to be who I am today. He passed away five days later.

"Learn to enjoy every minute of your life. Be happy now. Don't wait for something outside of yourself to make you happy in the future. Think how really precious is the time you have to spend, whether it's at work or with your family. Every minute should be enjoyed and savored."

- Earl Nightingale

Action Steps:

1. Write down 3 things you are grateful for today. No matter how small it is.

2. Think about at least, two living people who have made a positive impression on your life and thank them verbally in person. To take it to another level, handwrite them a letter of thanks. Mail them that letter or hand deliver it to them directly.

CHAPTER 7

Consistency & Commitment

"Let us not grow weary *or* become discouraged in doing good, for at the proper time we will reap if we do not give in."

- Galatians 6:9

No matter what you do, if you stay consistent at something, it will lead to a result. Whether the result is the desired one is up to what you are consistent at doing. Back in 2014, I had the idea of doing a podcast. Years went by, and after meandering around, I finally got a concept of what my podcast will be about. It was going to be a podcast that talks about books and music from underground artists that I like. After talking with some buddies of mine in the coaching business, I decided to modify and sharpen my concept even further to have it as a podcast where authors share their expertise, stories, and services to give them a platform for keeping them in the minds of their readers. Thus, the Going North Podcast was born!

After reaching episode 35 of the Going North Podcast, I received a podcast guest pitch email from a publicist of Interview Connections. When I saw the name of the guest, I was ecstatic. His name was Damion Lupo, a millionaire black belt martial arts master who founded Yogido, *a hybrid of Yoga and Aikido.* He's also the author of 4 books to boot! This email reassured me that I was doing something right because it reminded me of Nancy Gaines when she gave her advice to entrepreneurs on episode 8 of the Going North Podcast. Nancy's advice was, "When people start coming to you for help and business, you know you are on the right path."

I immediately thanked God for this because it was a sign that if I stay consistent and keep pushing forward, success is certain. I was ecstatic and full of gratitude after seeing this email. Especially, since it was the beginning of many inquiries from authors and their publicists. This led a weekly podcast to becoming a bi-weekly podcast that reaches listeners from all over the world.

"When I thought I couldn't go on, I forced myself to keep going. My success is based on persistence, not luck."

- Estee Lauder

Show up & Keep Showing Up!

Keep showing up. I let loss hit me like a ton of bricks. Some of those bricks ended up in my belly and the rest, in my mind and emotions. I stopped showing up as much to the gym; I stopped showing up to work (mentally), I stopped showing up in my prayer life. When you stop showing up, you cease heading north. I was heading east, west and side to side like a game of ping-pong. There is no off-season with success — only periods of rest for your clay vehicle called the human body.

Show up regularly. Continuous improvement does not live with continuous stagnation. Those who celebrate continuously after a victory ends up hindering the progress that led to that victory if they don't get back to work. Those who celebrate and try to make the celebration permanent, end up hindering the movement that created that celebration. Destination celebration happens over and over with destination continuation. Keep the foot on the gas, enter cruise control for a few miles and motivate yourself through silence, meditation and stillness so you can return to the gas pedal of action.

No one needs permission to have their own version of success, and no one needs to oversleep on the bed of yesterday's victories. Sleep is good but oversleeping is bad for your body. Don't oversleep on your bed made through your gifts and past victories by not using them. Don't oversleep on your bed made with past victories if you want more and greater victories. Sleep for the sake of top-level performance, not for the sake of sedentary stability.

Vulnerability is at its highest during an immediate victory. Have gratitude for your memories but seek to create more memories in your hourglass of life. Turn your grains of sand into bits of memorable experiences.

Comfort Poisons Progress

"When you are sick and tired of hearing something, you are just then beginning to get it."

- Mike Murdock

A while ago, I became sick and tired of hearing about getting out of my comfort zone. Getting out of your comfort zone requires you to do something new to break your routine and grow from that experience of getting out of your norm. The norm is normal because it's something done long enough to become a habitual routine. I was doing a routine to the point where I hated hearing about getting out of it. Little did I know that the above quote explained my frustration. Soon, when I did some things differently like giving speeches that were a little more personal and continuing my podcast that connects me with people all over the world, I soon did not mind hearing about the comfort zone. After a while, I finally "got it".

This book might not be the 1st of its kind that you may have read, but it shouldn't be the last one of its kind that you read either. Remember everything you can from this book and try to apply as much of it as you can because everything cannot be accomplished in one day, but one day of repetition multiplied can yield higher results in different areas of your life. Elite performance is a combination of rest, repetition, reward and reinvention. To keep yourself relevant, reinvent yourself and add to your mental arsenal. Decide today to repeat the things that yield positive results in your life. The reward of repetition is confidence. Confidence is the beginning of victories. Continue to stay the course and go north to your greatness.

"I fear not the man who has practiced ten thousand kicks once, but I fear the man who has practiced one kick ten thousand times."

- Bruce Lee

READ & GROW RICH: BOOKS ARE KNOWLEDGE CAVES HIDING SECRETS

"Books are the bastion of sustainable success and keys to the vehicle of a manifested dream."

- Dominique Brightmon

Books are the gatekeepers of knowledge, imagination and metaphorical time travel. Read the best books to get the best out of your life. Some books were written by others who put decades of research and experience into a low-cost package. A $25 book could contain 25 years of study and a string of life events that you could absorb in a few hours. Books are written by people who want to share something with others. Whether it is their expertise, experience, or examinations of life. In the 21st century, books are exponentially growing in terms of production but are containing things that are not entirely new.

Books are the clay that hides the gold. There's a story about a golden Buddha statue that was hidden beneath some clay because the Buddhist monks who originally owned the statue were being invaded and they wanted to protect it. The book cover is the clay, and the pages within it are the gold that can be mined and set aside for later. Decide to read more than ever before. Read more books every year if you can. Even re-read to find some stuff that you may have missed.

Action Steps

1. Read 3 Non-fiction books

2. Take 3 new total actions gained from those books

3. Write and or journal about your experience with executing those 3 actions.

In the last book, I named 100 books to advance yourself and amplify your life called the *100 Books for Dynamic Living*. Advancement doesn't stop! So here are 50 more books to keep fuel in your mental tank for a continuous flame of enduring success.

1. Action Has No Season by Mike Roberts

2. Fearless by Steve Chandler

3. The Winner's Lifestyle by Daniel Ally

4. The 55 Soft Skills That Guide Employee and Organizational Success by Dr. Tobin Porterfield & Bob Graham

5. The 7 Lost Secrets of Success by Joe Vitale

6. Inspired to Lead by Chris Jordan

7. The Greatness Manifesto by Marc "Greatness" Hunter

8. Reach Your Mountaintop by Jeff Davis

9. Daily Affirmations for African Americans by Dennis Kimbro

10. ABC's of Networking by Dr. Sinclair Grey III

11. The Wright Thought by Luke Wright

12. Hustle & Grow Rich by Tierca Berry

13. Re-Inventing Life by Damion Lupo

14. There's Always a Way by Tony Little

15. Creating Your Destiny by Patrick Snow

16. The Uncommon Leader by Mike Murdock

17. The Law of Recognition by Mike Murdock

18. Dig Your Well Before You're Thirsty by Harvey Mackay

19. Knockout Entrepreneur by George Foreman

20. Anything You Want by Derek Sivers

21. Key to Yourself by Venice Bloodworth

22. 15 Invaluable Laws of Growth by John Maxwell

23. Robert Schuller's Life Changers

24. Make It, So You Won't Have to Fake It by Patricia Fripp

25. 10 Pillars of Wealth by Alex Becker

26. You & Your Network by Fred Smith

27. Shoe Dog by Phil Knight

28. No Limits by John Maxwell

29. 50 Ways to Create Great Relationships by Steve Chandler

43. The 25 Biblical Laws of Success by Rubens Teixeira & William Douglas

44. Wealth Warrior by Steve Chandler

45. Community of Self by Na'im Akbar

46. The Best Year of Your Life by Debbie Ford

47. A Passion for Success by Kazuo Inamori

48. Elon Musk: Tesla, SpaceX, and the Quest for a Fantastic Future by Ashlee Vance

49. The Way of the Fight by Georges St. Pierre

50. The Go-Giver by Bob Burg

"Some good book is usually responsible for the success of every great man."

- Roy L. Smith

50 QUOTES FOR THE ELITE & IGNITED PERFORMER

1. "Elite performers know that broken focus will shatter productivity and hinder opportunities for victory." - Dominique Brightmon

2. "The willingness to do what needs to be done is one of the benchmarks of success." - Jacqueline Whitmore

3. "Life is too short to permit discouragers close to you." - Mike Murdock

4. "Anyone who doesn't make mistakes isn't trying hard enough." - Wess Roberts

5. "Great achievers have always understood the necessity of organized assistance." - Fred Smith

6. "We are not what we say, or how we feel, or what we think. *We are what we do.*" - Dr. Gordon Livingston

7. "The greatest danger occurs at the moment of victory" - Napoleon Bonaparte

8. "We must see ourselves as the source of all change. Otherwise, we will always be looking for someone else to make the change for us." - Anthony Robbins

9. "What the wise do in the beginning, fools do in the end." - Warren Buffett

10. "Without the strength to endure the crisis, one will not see the opportunity within; it is within the process of endurance that opportunity reveals itself." - Chin-Ning Chu

11. "The school of thought or the historical relevance make no difference to me. What matters to me is the practical application of the novel thinking." - Georges St. Pierre

12. "I'll take care of me for you and you take care of you for me."- Jim Rohn

13. "No matter what accomplishments you make, somebody helped you." - Althea Gibson

14. "As an entrepreneur, you are working for yourself. You are calling your own shots, determining your destiny. Truth is, even if someone else signs your paycheck, you are still in business for yourself. We all are!" - George Foreman

15. "One of the key aspects of emotional intelligence is knowing yourself: your strengths and your weaknesses. Feedback is the vehicle you can use to achieve that. Feedback is information about how you are showing up to others and in the world." - Lewis Howes

16. "Resistance builds strength - all resistance, in one form or another. We don't like resistance because it's difficult, but overcoming resistance is what makes us stronger." - Shawn Michaels

17. "You'll never change your life until you change something you do daily. The secret of your success is found in your daily routine." - John C. Maxwell

18. "Taking good care of yourself is not a form of self-indulgence. Self-care includes exercising

regularly, eating healthy foods, getting enough sleep, pursuing creative outlets, and knowing how to relax and let go." - Jacqueline Whitmore

19. "You gain strength, courage, and confidence by every experience in which you really stop to look fear in the face. You must do the thing which you think you cannot do." - Eleanor Roosevelt

20. "Once we effect a change, we should reinforce it immediately." - Anthony Robbins

21. "Celebrate your success and find humor in your failures. Don't take yourself so seriously. Loosen up and everyone else around you will loosen up. Have fun and always show enthusiasm. When all else fails, put on a costume and sing a silly song." - Sam Walton

22. "All your ideas may be solid or even good...But you have to actually EXECUTE on them for them to matter." - Gary Vaynerchuk

23. "The future is what brings today's choices into proper focus." - Andy Stanley

24. "While you're waiting for your purpose to drop down from heaven, do something." - Wendy Elover

25. "You don't need a lot of money to make a difference in the world." - Jeff Davis

26. "Find the parts of yourself that need to be updated." - Christopher Aitken

27. "Your job is not to solve all the problems in one day." - Christina Alva

28. "Setbacks teach you how to regroup, how to re-strategize and how to go get it." - Dr. Duane Mangum

29. "We overestimate the event and underestimate the process. Every fulfilled dream occurred because of dedication to a process." - John C. Maxwell

30. "As long as you can breathe you got a possibility of changing circumstances in your life." - Avon Bellamy

31. "You don't have to be the best to put out your best." - Jon Michail

32. "Asking for help is not a sign of weakness; it is evidence of wisdom." - Andy Stanley

33. "Emulate the great." - Unknown

34. "It's better to hang out with people better than you. Pick out associates whose behavior is better than yours and you'll drift in that direction." - Warren Buffett

35. "Stamina, will, courage and self-confidence distinguish winners from losers." - Wess Roberts

36. "Leaders are paid to lead on bad days, not to abdicate when challenged - and not to take credit for easy victories." - Wess Roberts

37. "If you don't see yourself as a winner, then you cannot perform as a winner." - Zig Ziglar

38. "Don't wait for extraordinary opportunities. Seize common occasions and make them great!" - Og Mandino

39. "Enjoy whatever you do, but avoid complacency. Remember that you will never become highly accomplished in activities you do not enjoy." - Wess Roberts

40. "Tomorrow is the busiest day of the week." - Spanish Proverb

41. "Value = Strengths + Actions + Results" - P. Anthony Burnham

42. "Worry can lead to physical drain, illness, psychological turmoil, and damage to interpersonal relationships." - Charles Manz

43. "Mastery is not about perfection. It's about a process, a journey. The master is the one who stays on the path day after day, year after year. The master is the one who is willing to try, and fail, and try again, for as long as he or she lives." - George Leonard

44. "The key to triumph is for you to *try*. Successful people are decisive and they try far more things than other people do." - Brian Tracy

45. "Use your mind in ways that serve you and quicken your growth." - Laura Bushnell

46. "Talk of those things that will make people the better for listening to you. Thus you will infect them with health and strength and not with weakness and disease." - Ralph Waldo Trine

47. "Change the habit of getting ready for life in favor of getting on with it now." - Patricia Ryan Madson

48. "What you refuse to master today will master you tomorrow." - Mike Murdock

49. "If you are in a really successful place right now, stay aware, stay current, and keep your eyes on the next thing you are going to do to maintain your success." - Larry Winget

50. "When God closes my eyes for the last time, I want people to be talking about something that I did one hundred years from now." - Reginald Gant

NOTES

Chapter 1

1. Forbes' Company Listings
   https://www.forbes.com/companies/
   toyota-motor/#5ae7485952bd

Chapter 5

1. 2008 Sleep, Performance and the Workplace
   https://www.sleepfoundation.
   org/professionals/sleep-america-
   polls/2008-sleep-performance-and-workplace

2. Article: 20 Crazy Health Benefits of Laughter—
   No Joke!
   https://bestlifeonline.com/
   health-benefits-laughter/

Made in the USA
Middletown, DE
15 March 2022